S0-AZS-652

OCEANS OF AIR

AUTHORS

Mary Atwater
The University of Georgia

Prentice Baptiste
University of Houston

Lucy Daniel
Rutherford County Schools

Jay Hackett
University of Northern Colorado

Richard Moyer
University of Michigan

Carol Takemoto
Los Angeles Unified School District

Nancy Wilson
Sacramento Unified School District

Inland Passage, Alaska

Macmillan/McGraw-Hill School Publishing Company
New York   Columbus

MACMILLAN / McGRAW-HILL

SCIENCE TURNS MINDS ON™

CONSULTANTS

Assessment:

Janice M. Camplin
Curriculum Coordinator, Elementary Science
Mentor, Western New York
Lake Shore Central Schools
Angola, NY

Mary Hamm
Associate Professor
Department of Elementary Education
San Francisco State University
San Francisco, CA

Cognitive Development:

Dr. Elisabeth Charron
Assistant Professor of Science Education
Montana State University
Bozeman, MT

Sue Teele
Director of Education Extension
University of California, Riverside
Riverside, CA

Cooperative Learning:

Harold Pratt
Executive Director of Curriculum
Jefferson County Public Schools
Golden, CO

Earth Science:

Thomas A. Davies
Research Scientist
The University of Texas
Austin, TX

David G. Futch
Associate Professor of Biology
San Diego State University
San Diego, CA

Dr. Shadia Rifai Habbal
Harvard-Smithsonian Center for Astrophysics
Cambridge, MA

Tom Murphree, Ph.D.
Global Systems Studies
Monterey, CA

Suzanne O'Connell
Assistant Professor
Wesleyan University
Middletown, CT

Environmental Education:

Cheryl Charles, Ph.D.
Executive Director
Project Wild
Boulder, CO

Gifted:

Sandra N. Kaplan
Associate Director, National/State Leadership
Training Institute on the Gifted/Talented
Ventura County Superintendent of Schools Office
Northridge, CA

Global Education:

M. Eugene Gilliom
Professor of Social Studies and Global Education
The Ohio State University
Columbus, OH

Merry M. Merryfield
Assistant Professor of Social Studies and Global
Education
The Ohio State University
Columbus, OH

Intermediate Specialist

Sharon L. Strating
Missouri State Teacher of the Year
Northwest Missouri State University
Marysville, MO

Life Science:

Carl D. Barrentine
Associate Professor of Biology
California State University
Bakersfield, CA

V.L. Holland
Professor and Chair, Biological Sciences
Department
California Polytechnic State University
San Luis Obispo, CA

Donald C. Lisowy
Education Specialist
New York, NY

Dan B. Walker
Associate Dean for Science Education and
Professor of Biology
San Jose State University
San Jose, CA

Literature:

Dr. Donna E. Norton
Texas A&M University
College Station, TX

Tina Thoburn, Ed.D.
President
Thoburn Educational Enterprises, Inc.
Ligonier, PA

Macmillan/McGraw-Hill School Division
10 Union Square East
New York, New York 10003

Printed in the United States of America

ISBN 0-02-276119-5 / 4

    3 4 5 6 7 8 9 VHJ 99 98 97 96 95

Cumulus clouds

Mathematics:
Martin L. Johnson
Professor, Mathematics Education
University of Maryland at College Park
College Park, MD

Physical Science:
Max Diem, Ph.D.
Professor of Chemistry
City University of New York, Hunter College
New York, NY

Gretchen M. Gillis
Geologist
Maxus Exploration Company
Dallas, TX

Wendell H. Potter
Associate Professor of Physics
Department of Physics
University of California, Davis
Davis, CA

Claudia K. Viehland
Educational Consultant, Chemist
Sigma Chemical Company
St. Louis, MO

Reading:
Jean Wallace Gillet
Reading Teacher
Charlottesville Public Schools
Charlottesville, VA

Charles Temple, Ph. D.
Associate Professor of Education
Hobart and William Smith Colleges
Geneva, NY

Safety:
Janice Sutkus
Program Manager: Education
National Safety Council
Chicago, IL

Science Technology and Society (STS):
William C. Kyle, Jr.
Director, School Mathematics and Science Center
Purdue University
West Lafayette, IN

Social Studies:
Mary A. McFarland
Instructional Coordinator of
Social Studies, K-12, and
Director of Staff Development
Parkway School District
St. Louis, MO

Students Acquiring English:
Mrs. Bronwyn G. Frederick, M.A.
Bilingual Teacher
Pomona Unified School District
Pomona, CA

Misconceptions:
Dr. Charles W. Anderson
Michigan State University
East Lansing, MI

Dr. Edward L. Smith
Michigan State University
East Lansing, MI

Multicultural:
Bernard L. Charles
Senior Vice President
Quality Education for Minorities Network
Washington, DC

Cheryl Willis Hudson
Graphic Designer and Publishing Consultant
Part Owner and Publisher, Just Us Books, Inc.
Orange, NJ

Paul B. Janeczko
Poet
Hebron, MA

James R. Murphy
Math Teacher
La Guardia High School
New York, NY

Ramon L. Santiago
Professor of Education and Director of ESL
Lehman College, City University of New York
Bronx, NY

Clifford E. Trafzer
Professor and Chair, Ethnic Studies
University of California, Riverside
Riverside, CA

STUDENT ACTIVITY TESTERS
Jennifer Kildow
Brooke Straub
Cassie Zistl
Betsy McKeown
Seth McLaughlin
Max Berry
Wayne Henderson

FIELD TEST TEACHERS
Sharon Ervin
San Pablo Elementary School
Jacksonville, FL

Michelle Gallaway
Indianapolis Public School #44
Indianapolis, IN

Kathryn Gallman
#7 School
Rochester, NY

Karla McBride
#44 School
Rochester, NY

Diane Pease
Leopold Elementary
Madison, WI

Kathy Perez
Martin Luther King Elementary
Jacksonville, FL

Ralph Stamler
Thoreau School
Madison, WI

Joanne Stern
Hilltop Elementary School
Glen Burnie, MD

Janet Young
Indianapolis Public School #90
Indianapolis, IN

CONTRIBUTING WRITER
Jim Gorman

OCEANS OF AIR

Activities!

Features

Departments

Oceans of Air

Think about the people who lived hundreds of years ago. What did they know about the weather? How did they learn about storms? What if you had lived many years ago and had no one to explain the weather to you? What would you think about thunder? What would you do if you were outdoors in a snowstorm? Would knowing about weather be important to you?

Minds On! There are lots of ways to describe snow—wet snow, falling snow, soft snow, snow crystals, and drifting snow, for example. Close your eyes and think of rain. How would you describe it? What would you call a gentle rain, or a spring rain, or a heavy rain? With a partner, think of five different ways to describe rain. Make up a word for each description. Share your rain vocabulary with your class. ●

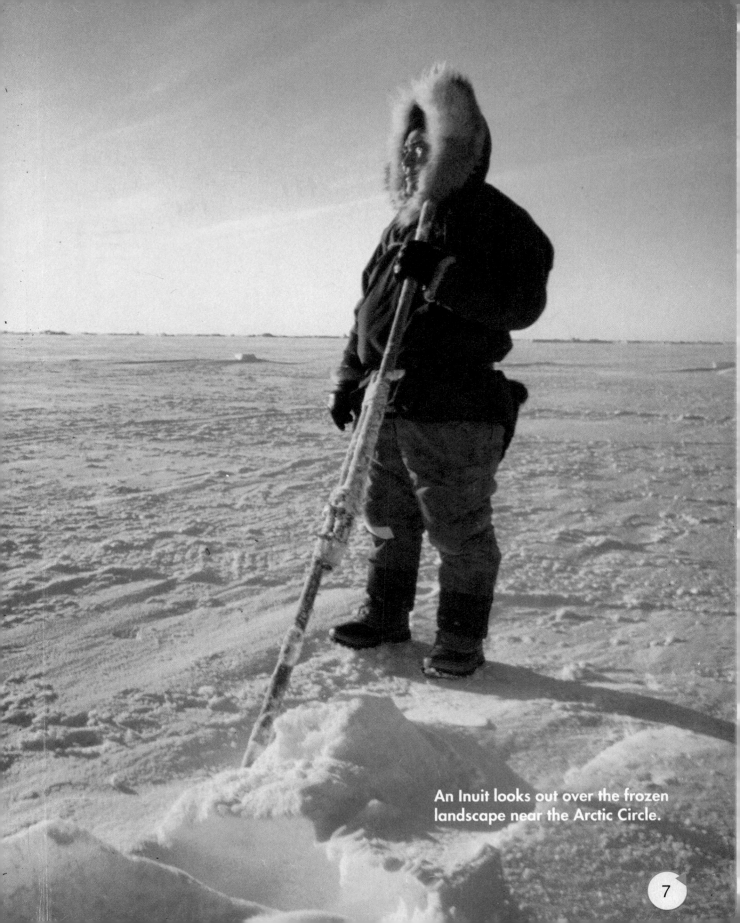

An Inuit looks out over the frozen landscape near the Arctic Circle.

Long ago, people learned about storms by watching the skies for signs. Clouds, wind, and the way animals behaved before a storm helped teach people to prepare for bad weather.

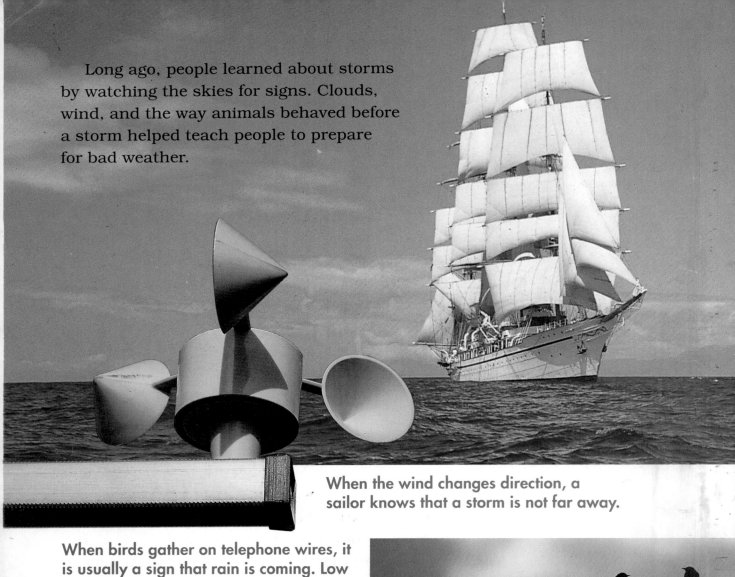

When the wind changes direction, a sailor knows that a storm is not far away.

When birds gather on telephone wires, it is usually a sign that rain is coming. Low air pressure makes it difficult for birds to fly.

Some people say that a cricket can tell you the temperature. Count a cricket's chirps in 15 seconds. Add 37. The answer will be the temperature.

You may want to check a thermometer to see how accurate you are.

Today, weather forecasters check the temperature of the air, the speed and direction of the wind, and the amount of moisture in the air to predict what kind of weather is coming.

In this unit you'll find out how to use the signs around you as well as scientific instruments to predict weather.

Minds On! "Red sky at night, sailor's delight. Red sky at morning, sailor take warning." This is an old folk saying. It predicts clear weather if the sunset is bright. But if the sky is red in the morning, it predicts a storm. Ask your family if they know of other folk sayings that predict the weather. Share what you've learned with your classmates. ●

Science in Literature

People have always been curious about the weather, especially storms. Does watching a storm of any kind make you shiver with excitement? Reading about weather and storms can be just as interesting as watching them. Here are some fascinating books about storms, hurricanes, and tornadoes that you might enjoy reading.

Hurricane!
by Faith McNulty.
New York: Harper and Row, 1983.

John helps his parents prepare for a New England hurricane. He learns to observe weather signs from animals, birds, and the sky. These signs tell him that a big storm is coming. John observes from the safety of his home but worries about his tree house in the big, old tree outside his back door. Will they both outlast the storm? Look for signs of the approaching hurricane as you read this book.

Weather
by Howard E. Smith, Jr.
New York: Doubleday, 1990.

Everything you have ever wanted to know about weather is in this book. You can read about blizzards, dust storms, hurricanes, and tornadoes. You'll be amazed when you read about the problems that happen when fog and pollution combine. If you are concerned about Earth's future, you'll be interested in reading about future climates.

Other Good Books To Read

The Science Book of Air
by Neil Ardley.
New York: Harcourt Brace Jovanovich, 1991.

This book has wonderful experiments that are easy and fun to do. Discover all the properties of air for yourself and amaze your friends, too!

Tornado Alert
by Franklin M. Branley.
New York: Thomas Y. Crowell, 1988.

What is a tornado? How do you know a tornado is coming? How dangerous can this storm be? Would you know how to protect yourself if you heard a tornado warning? Read this book to find out more about the funnel-shaped storm we call a tornado.

The Mystery of the Double Double
Cross by Mary Blount Christian.
Niles, IL: Albert Whitman and Company, 1982.

Jeff gets kidnapped by mistake and finds himself in the middle of a terrible hurricane. Read this book to find out more about Jeff's adventure. How does he survive the hurricane and his kidnappers?

Storms by Seymour Simon.
New York: Morrow Junior Books, 1989.

Did you know that there are about 16 million thunderstorms around the world each year? If you want to read about thunderstorms, tornadoes, and hurricanes, this book is for you!

Getting in Touch With Air

Do you like riddles? Try this one. What has no color, no taste, and no smell but can sometimes knock you off your feet? Discover the answer in this lesson.

People and animals need air because their bodies need oxygen and other gases to live. You could live without food or water for several days, but you would live only minutes without air.

Air is invisible, but you can see that it takes up space when a balloon expands as you blow it up. You can see air rippling the grass and whipping the oceans into white-capped waves. You can't smell air, but odors of every kind reach your nose by currents of air.

Air is made up of about one-fifth oxygen and four-fifths nitrogen.

There are also small amounts of other gases, including water vapor and carbon dioxide. Air allows plants and animals to exchange the oxygen and carbon dioxide that living things need to survive.

Air can work for us in other ways, too. The jackhammer that breaks up concrete and a dentist's drill are powered by air. Air bags are used in cars to protect drivers and passengers.

Minds On! In your *Activity Log* on page 1, write two ways you can prove that air is around you. Compare your ideas with those of a classmate.●

Having fun with a giant
soap bubble

Activity!

Making Magic With Air

You and your classmates could come up with a long list of evidence proving that air is everywhere. The following activities will offer even more evidence.

What You Need

string   jar

Activity Log pages 2-3

water

2 balloons

straight pin

plastic shoe box

cardboard

paper towels

metric ruler

scissors

What To Do

Part A

1 Fill the plastic box half full of water.

2 Crumble a paper towel and place it in the jar.

3 Predict what will happen when the jar is put upside down in the water.

4 Hold the jar with the open end down and push it straight down to the bottom of the plastic box without tilting it. Record your observations.

Safety!

See the *Safety Tip* in step 3 of Part C.

Part B

1 Cut a square from the cardboard larger than the diameter of the plastic jar.

2 Fill the jar half full of water. Place the cut section of the cardboard over the mouth of the jar.

3 Predict what will happen when the jar is turned upside down.

4 Flip the jar over as you hold the cardboard in place. Now take your hand off the cardboard. Record what happens.

Part C

1 Tie an inflated balloon to each end of a metric ruler. Tie a string to the middle of the ruler. Hold the string so that the ruler is suspended. Move the balloons in or out to balance the ruler.

2 Predict what will happen if one balloon is popped.

3 Using a straight pin, pop one balloon. *Safety Tip:* Be careful when using the straight pin.

What Happened?

1. Compare your predictions with your observations in each part of the activity. How accurate were you?

2. In Part A, why doesn't water fill up the glass and get the paper wet?

3. Were you surprised at the results in Part B? How can you explain what did happen?

4. In Part C, which end of the ruler dropped? What property of air caused this to happen?

What Now?

1. Which property of air causes your ears to pop?

2. Which property of air helps you keep a bicycle tire inflated?

EXPLORE

15

The Properties of Air

Space

Were you surprised by any part of the Explore Activity? You know that air is matter. It has all the properties of matter. Did you believe that the air would keep water from flowing into the jar? Just like other matter, air took up the space in the jar and kept the water out.

Mass

Another property of matter is mass. Air also has mass. The inflated balloon in the Explore Activity was heavier than the empty, popped balloon. Which balloon had more matter? Which balloon had more mass?

Blimp

CAREERS Blimp Pilot

If you have ever watched sports on TV, you've probably seen a view of the stadium from a blimp. **Blimps** are giant balloons that are filled with helium to make them lighter than air. To be a blimp pilot, you need a blimp license and you should like to travel.

Activity!

Massive Amounts of Air

To help you understand that air has mass, let's do the balloon part of the Explore Activity in a different way.

What You Need
balloon, balance, *Activity Log* page 4

Compare an empty balloon with one that is full of air. Do they have the same mass? First, use a balance to measure the mass of a balloon before it's inflated. Blow as much air into it as you can without breaking it. Use the balance to measure the mass of the balloon with the air inside. Subtract the mass of the empty balloon from the mass of the balloon with air. What is the mass of the air you breathed into the balloon?

Pressure

Like all matter, air has mass and takes up space. You can see how much space it takes up when you blow up a balloon. The difference in measurement between the empty balloon and the inflated balloon is the mass of the air. Now you will discover that air exerts pressure.

Minds On! Imagine you were at the bottom of a pile of feathers 10 meters (about 33 feet) deep. Would the feathers feel heavy to you? The pressure of the feathers would not push you down. Predict what you would feel if the feathers were piled up to 10 kilometers (about 6 miles). On the surface of Earth, you are at the bottom of a layer of air that is hundreds of kilometers deep. The weight of air pushing down on Earth's surface is **air pressure** (âr presh´ ər).

Activity!

Air Power

Did you know that you can lift heavy objects with air?

What You Need

plastic sandwich bag, plastic drinking straw, tape, textbook, *Activity Log* page 5

Tape one end of the straw into the open end of the sandwich bag. Be sure the tape completely seals around the straw. You don't want any air passing in or out of the bag except through the straw. Set the bag under your textbook.

Blow into the straw with a steady, even breath. What do you notice about the book as you blow? Which of air's properties caused the change you saw? Record your observations or draw a picture of what you have just done in your *Activity Log.*

You saw how much power air has when it lifted your textbook. Rescue workers use air to lift a bus that has collided with a car.

If we measure air pressure at high altitudes, it is lower than at Earth's surface. Gravity holds most of Earth's air close to the surface. Gravity is less as you move farther from Earth's surface. If you go to higher altitudes, for example when you fly up in an airplane, there is less air above you so you feel less air pressure.

You have felt the change in air pressure if you have taken an elevator to the top of a tall building or flown in an airplane. Now that you know that air pressure is lower at high altitudes, can you explain why your ears pop on such rides?

The mercury barometer measures air pressure by using a hollow tube filled with mercury. Most weather stations and research laboratories use this barometer for accuracy.

The aneroid barometer also measures air pressure and is most often used in people's homes.

As the skydiver falls closer to Earth, the air pressure will increase.

The Atmosphere

Earth is surrounded by air just as your bed is covered by a blanket. This blanket of air is called the **atmosphere** (at´ məs fîr´). Earth's atmosphere includes four layers. These layers have distinct characteristics.

The Northern Lights

In the high altitudes of the northern hemisphere, there is a natural light show that can be seen most easily at night. This display is called the **Northern Lights.** Sometimes the lights move or flicker far across the atmosphere for thousands of kilometers. The lights are usually blue-green, but sometimes they appear red or purple. There are similar lights in the high latitudes of the southern hemisphere called the Southern Lights.

The Northern and Southern Lights are the most visible evidence of the sun's effect on Earth's atmosphere.

Northern Lights

Ozone layer

weather balloon

cumulonimbus

Earth

The **exosphere** (ek´ sō sfîr´) is about 900 kilometers (about 560 miles) high. It is found at the edge of space.

weather satellite

meteors

These two sections of the atmosphere are often grouped together as the **thermosphere**.

The **ionosphere** (ī on´ ə sfîr´) is an upper layer of the atmosphere and is about 480 kilometers (about 298 miles) high. The air is very thin and there is very little gas in this layer.

The **mesosphere** (mez´ ə sfîr´) is the layer between 50 and 80 kilometers (about 50 miles) above the surface of Earth.

weather plane

cirrus

The **stratosphere** (strat´ ə sfîr´) extends from the troposphere to about 50 kilometers (about 31 miles) above the surface of Earth. This is where transcontinental jet aircraft fly. It contains a region called the ozone layer, which absorbs ultraviolet rays from the sun.

The layer closest to Earth is called the **troposphere** (trop´ ə sfîr´). This is the layer that contains the air and water that living things on Earth need to survive. The troposphere reaches to a height of about 13 kilometers (about 8 miles). The weather we experience in our everyday lives takes place in the troposphere.

Global Warming

Our atmosphere traps some of the solar energy that strikes Earth. We call this the **greenhouse effect**, and it helps keep Earth warm. One gas that helps trap this energy is carbon dioxide. If the amount of carbon dioxide increases, then we would expect the atmosphere to trap more heat. This would be an increase in the greenhouse effect, and it could cause Earth to get warmer. A worldwide increase in Earth's temperatures would be called **global warming**.

The glass or plastic of a greenhouse lets in sunlight. Some of the light is changed to energy that can't pass back through the glass, and this energy heats up the greenhouse.

Heat from sun

Excess heat escapes

Heat reflected

Heat reflected

Excess heat escapes

Excess heat escapes

Heat reflected

Excess heat escapes

Excess heat escapes

Heat reflected

Excess heat escapes

Heat from sun

Atmosphere

Heat reflected

Heat reflected

Heat reflected

Excess heat escapes

Earth's atmosphere acts like a greenhouse. It lets in the sun's energy and holds some of it. When too much energy is held in, the temperatures around the world will rise.

Minds On! What do you think would happen if Earth became warmer? Make a list of five good things and five problems that could happen as a result of global warming. ●

Much of the increase in carbon dioxide is caused by burning. People burn fuels in their automobiles, airplanes, and buses. Carbon dioxide also increases when there are fewer plants to take it out of the air. One method of clearing land for farming is to cut down all the trees and then burn the small plants that are left. In what two ways does this add carbon dioxide to the air?

Plant a tree to help absorb carbon dioxide. It will provide Earth with more oxygen.

Sum It Up

Think of air as an invisible blanket that surrounds Earth. We call this the atmosphere. You can't see air, but you have proved that it is around you by investigating air's three properties. It has mass, it takes up space, and it exerts pressure. What else do you know about air? Just how important is it? Can you take air for granted?

Excess heat escapes

Recycle aluminum cans, glass bottles, plastic products, and newspapers instead of throwing them away. It takes less energy to produce a new product from recycled materials.

Critical Thinking

1. Why is air pressure higher near Earth's surface than at altitudes farther away from Earth?

2. Why do your ears pop when you ride up or down in a fast elevator?

3. You have learned about three properties of air. Think of each property and give an example of each one that you use every day.

When you go to the grocery store, take a canvas or string bag with you.

Why Does the Wind Blow?

Have you felt the wind in your face or watched branches on a tree sway in the breeze?
What causes the wind to blow?
Why is the wind stronger on one day than it is on another?

About 500 years ago, seafarers were just beginning to understand how to find steady winds that always blew in the same direction. They gave names to these steady winds and marked them on charts, much as we mark highways on maps today.

In this lesson you'll learn what causes wind, how scientists measure wind speed and determine wind direction, and how people use wind for work and play. In the next activity, you'll build an instrument for measuring wind speed.

Minds On! An international sign that warns residents who live near a coastal area that a hurricane is coming is two square red flags. The flags have black squares in the middle, and they fly one on top of the other. In the United States, these flags are flown from Coast Guard stations. Think of a flag that would warn people about dangerous wind conditions in your area. Where would you display this flag? Compare your idea with that of a classmate. ●

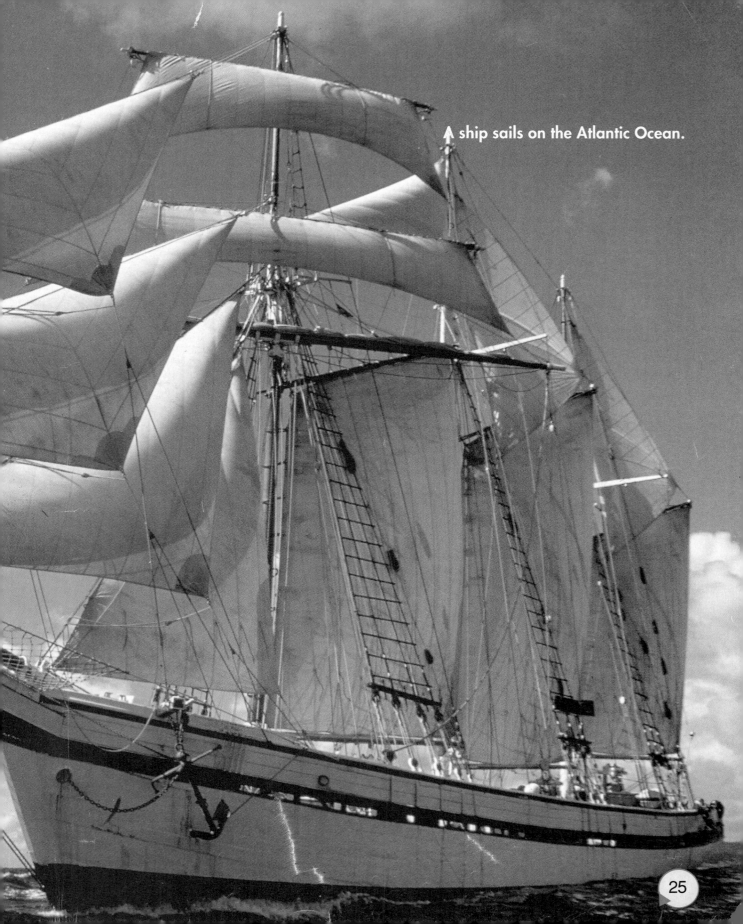

A ship sails on the Atlantic Ocean.

Activity!

Can You Measure Wind Speed?

Have you ever thought about how fast the wind blows on a very windy day? In the following activity, you will build an instrument that will measure the speed of the wind.

centimeter ruler

watch   marker   scissors

What You Need

2 cardboard strips

straight pin   pencil

Activity Log pages 6-7

tape

paper cups

What To Do

1 Measure one line 8 centimeters long on one side of each cup. With scissors cut through the line on each cup. Cut carefully. *Safety Tip:* Always use scissors carefully.

2 Mark one cup with a large black **X** on the opposite side of its slit.

See the *Safety Tips* in steps 1 and 5.

3 Make a plus sign with the strips of cardboard and tape them together.

4 Slide each cardboard strip's end through a cup's slit to the opposite side. Tape this end securely to the inside of the cup. All cups should face the same direction.

5 Push the straight pin through the center of the cardboard plus sign and into the eraser on the pencil. *Safety Tip:* Be careful when using the straight pin.

6 Draw a map of the schoolyard.

7 Holding on to the pencil securely, carry your device into the schoolyard. Observe what happens at four different locations. Choose locations near and away from buildings.

8 At each of the four locations that you have marked on your map, count the number of times the cup marked with the **X** spins past the holder's arm in 30 seconds. This number divided by 3 will give the approximate wind speed in kilometers per hour. Write down the wind speed at each of the four locations on your map.

What Happened?

1. At which location did the wind blow the strongest?

2. At which location did the wind blow the least?

What Now?

1. Why do you think the wind speed was different in some of the locations where you tested your instrument?

2. List five activities or jobs that might be easier to do when the wind is blowing.

EXPLORE

Which Way Does the Wind Blow?

In the Explore Activity, you made a weather instrument called an **anemometer** (an´ ə mom´ i tər). Your anemometer probably showed you that winds blew more briskly in certain locations. You might go to the same place tomorrow and find the wind blowing from another direction. Maybe the wind will not be as strong. Why does the wind have so little force one day and so much the next? To answer this question, you will need to learn more about temperature and air pressure. Differences in temperature and air pressure and the way they act together cause wind. **Wind** is the horizontal movement of air across Earth's surface.

Wind vanes point toward the direction from which the wind is blowing.

The water in the pool warms up more slowly than the land. It also cools more slowly. In the morning the water in the pool may be warmer than the concrete around the pool, because it has cooled more slowly during the night.

Activity!

Warming Up Fast or Slow

Try this activity to see if land really warms up more quickly than water.

What You Need

2 plastic boxes, water, sand, plastic jar, 2 thermometers, *Activity Log* page 8

Place the two plastic boxes on the window sill where they will receive direct sunlight. Fill one box with a jar of sand and the other with a jar of water. Place a thermometer in each box every 10 minutes for a period of 30 minutes. Record the temperature in your ***Activity Log.*** In which material did the temperature rise faster? Now think about the air above the material. Predict which material would have warmer air above it. What does this activity show you about how the air above different surfaces on Earth is warmed?

Why Breezes Blow

How do different temperatures in air cause wind? As air warms, its molecules move farther away from one another. If the molecules are farther apart, the air pressure is not as great. As air cools, the molecules move closer together. We say the air is **dense.** The more dense the air becomes, the more the pressure increases.

As the air gets warmer, it becomes less dense. It also has lower pressure than the air above the water.

The air above the shore also warms.

Winds form when the sun warms a surface, such as a shore near the ocean.

Winds begin to blow when cooler, more dense ocean air rushes in and pushes the warmer, less dense air up.

This cooler air is like the air let out of a balloon. It moves to an area of lower pressure. What do you think happens at night when the land becomes cooler than the water?

People have tried to control the wind for many reasons. Some people have used wind for transportation. Others use it to help make jobs easier. There are also some sports that use the wind.

Sailing for One

Focus on Technology

One wind sport that's become more popular in recent years is windsurfing. In addition to strong muscles and excellent swimming skills, you need an understanding of wind speed and direction to wind surf.

The person aboard grips a curved bar that moves the sail in any direction to take advantage of the wind.

The sail is triangular and mounted on a mast that can tip and rotate. The sail uses the wind and helps steer the windsurfer.

A sailboard looks like a surfboard with a sail. One person rides it standing up.

Windmills in Holland were used to pump water from fields.

Wind Energy for the Future

As fuel supplies, such as coal, oil, and natural gas, become scarce and more expensive, people are again turning to an old source of energy. Wind machines are being used more and more.

Wind is a good source of energy for several reasons. First, energy from the wind is free, as long as you can catch it. Second, it is clean energy because it does not cause pollution. In areas where strong winds blow regularly, as in some valleys and deserts of California, the wind has become a reliable source of energy.

Sum It Up

From a soft, gentle breeze to a powerful hurricane, the wind is a part of everyday life. The wind can be a valuable resource when it is used to make jobs easier. Understanding how temperature and pressure work together to cause wind is important to understanding cycles in the atmosphere. In the next lesson, you'll discover how wind helps create weather patterns.

Critical Thinking

1. How does the sun affect the land and water to create wind?
2. Explain why winds near a large body of water blow toward the land during the daytime and toward the water at night.
3. Explain three ways wind could be used to do work.

Today's wind machines look like the windmills of old but are called wind turbines. Large blades collect the wind, and the turbine changes it into electricity.

Most of the wind energy collected is collected in California.

Windfarm, Altamont Pass, California, United States

How Does a Cloud Form?

Water is on Earth in lakes, rivers, oceans, and glaciers. After it rains we often see water in puddles. But a day or two after a rainstorm, the water in puddles has disappeared. Where does this water go?

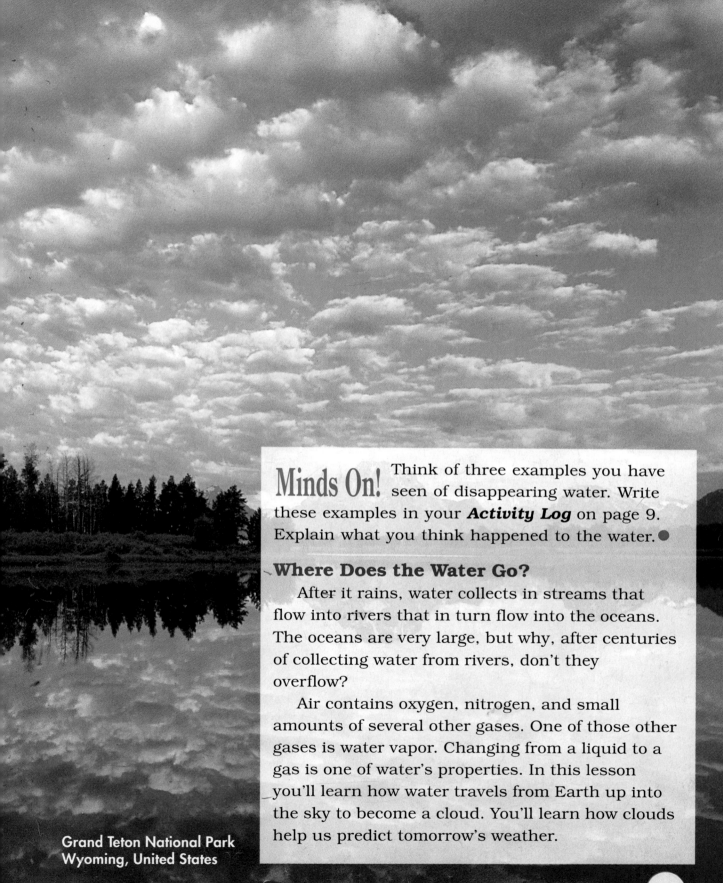

Minds On! Think of three examples you have seen of disappearing water. Write these examples in your *Activity Log* on page 9. Explain what you think happened to the water. ●

Where Does the Water Go?

After it rains, water collects in streams that flow into rivers that in turn flow into the oceans. The oceans are very large, but why, after centuries of collecting water from rivers, don't they overflow?

Air contains oxygen, nitrogen, and small amounts of several other gases. One of those other gases is water vapor. Changing from a liquid to a gas is one of water's properties. In this lesson you'll learn how water travels from Earth up into the sky to become a cloud. You'll learn how clouds help us predict tomorrow's weather.

Grand Teton National Park
Wyoming, United States

Activity!

What Makes a Cloud?

A cloud may look fluffy and dry like cotton candy, but actually it is a million floating drops of water and, sometimes, ice crystals. How are clouds made?

What You Need

Activity Log pages 10-11

paper towel

watch

water

ice

jar or clear plastic cup

What To Do

1 Wet the paper towel and wipe some water on the chalkboard. Watch the water, then record what happens to it in your *Activity Log.*

2 Half fill the jar with water. Look at the outside of the jar and then describe how it looks in your *Activity Log.*

3 Now add ice to fill the jar.

4 Continue to observe the jar. On the chart in your *Activity Log*, record changes that occur on the outside of the jar every 10 minutes for 30 minutes.

What Happened?

1. What did you see when you wiped the chalkboard with water?

2. What did you observe after you poured the water into the jar?

3. What about after you added the ice to the jar?

What Now?

1. Explain what happened to the water that was on the chalkboard.

2. Think back to the jar of ice and water—where did the water on the outside of the jar come from?

3. Some of the water on the outside of the jar was so heavy that it dripped down the jar. A ring or puddle formed around the jar on the table. Predict what would happen to the water in the puddle if you left it for two days. Record your prediction.

EXPLORE

The Water Cycle

In the Explore Activity, you saw water change from a liquid to a gas in the process called **evaporation** (i vap´ ə rā´ shən). The gas state of water is called water vapor. This is what happened when the water disappeared.

Adding ice to the water cooled the water and the jar. The water vapor near the jar cooled, also. It changed into water droplets. Changing from a gas to a liquid is called **condensation** (kon´ den sā´ shən). The droplets collected on the jar and clung to the sides. When the droplets became heavy and slid down the side of the jar, you saw another stage of the water cycle. **Precipitation** (pri sip´ i tā´ shən) happens when water falls from the sky in the form of rain, snow, hail, or sleet.

In Earth's water cycle, the sun is the energy source that causes evaporation.

Water condenses to form **clouds** of water droplets or ice particles suspended in the air.

The **water cycle** is the repeating cycle of evaporation, condensation, and precipitation that occurs on Earth.

The oceans do not overflow because water evaporates from them.

Rivers carry millions of liters of water into the oceans every day.

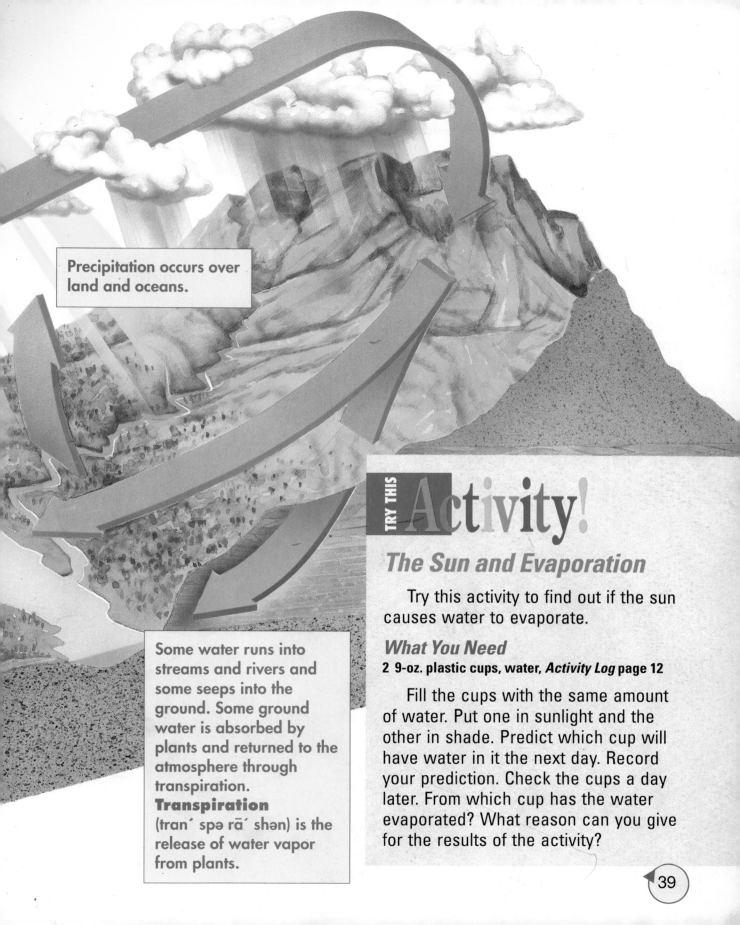

Precipitation occurs over land and oceans.

Some water runs into streams and rivers and some seeps into the ground. Some ground water is absorbed by plants and returned to the atmosphere through transpiration.
Transpiration
(tran´ spə rā´ shən) is the release of water vapor from plants.

TRY THIS Activity!

The Sun and Evaporation

Try this activity to find out if the sun causes water to evaporate.

What You Need
2 9-oz. plastic cups, water, *Activity Log* page 12

Fill the cups with the same amount of water. Put one in sunlight and the other in shade. Predict which cup will have water in it the next day. Record your prediction. Check the cups a day later. From which cup has the water evaporated? What reason can you give for the results of the activity?

Minds On! You have been in a cloud-making chamber if you have ever taken a warm bath on a cold day. Once you've filled the tub with warm water, what do you see rising out of the water? What forms on the cold surfaces in the room, such as a mirror, a window, or tile walls? Describe the parts of the water cycle and where they are occurring in the bathroom. ●

The bathtub example shows us how water travels back to the air from the oceans. Ocean water is warmed by the sun until it evaporates and rises. High in the atmosphere, the air temperature is cooler, like the air temperature in your bathroom. Warm water vapor in the air condenses, or changes back into its liquid form, just as water vapor in the bathroom condensed on the mirror, window, or walls. The sun provides heat to cause evaporation. Where does the heat go?

The warm bath water evaporates and condenses to form water droplets because the air in the bathroom is cool and low in moisture.

Activity!

Cooling Off

In this activity you will discover where the heat goes.

What You Need

2 thermometers, wet paper towel, cardboard fan, *Activity Log* page 13

Record the temperatures of the two thermometers in your ***Activity Log.*** Then, wrap the wet paper towel around the bulb of one thermometer. Leave the bulb of the other thermometer uncovered. Next, fan the bulbs of both thermometers with a cardboard fan for two minutes. Observe and record the temperatures of the thermometers. How did the temperatures change? Explain how a fan works to cool you on a hot summer day.

Health Link

Nature's Air Conditioner

What happens when you run or play really hard? Do you sweat? Sweating helps cool you. Sweat evaporates from your skin and cools you just as the thermometer in the activity was cooled. When sweat evaporates, heat leaves your body and goes into the air.

41

Clouds

Have you ever been out and about on a foggy morning? Did it seem as if you had your head in the clouds? Actually you did, since fog is a cloud that has formed close to the ground. Fog is formed the same way as all other clouds are formed. When warm, moist air cools, the water vapor in the air condenses. When many millions of droplets form together, we see a cloud. In the case of fog, the warm, moist air cooled close to the ground instead of high in the atmosphere.

Cumulus (kū′ myə ləs) clouds are large, thick, and puffy. They often look white with gray centers. Cumulus clouds are usually flat on the bottom and pile up to look like a dome. These clouds often form on hot summer days and sometimes turn into thunderclouds or thunderheads. When this happens, rain or thunderstorms may occur.

Cirrus (sir′ əs) clouds are made of tiny ice crystals. They are thin and white with feathery edges. They are the highest clouds in the sky and are seen when the weather is cool and dry.

Stratus (stra´ təs) clouds form at low altitudes. They can hold a lot of moisture and spread across the sky in flat, gray layers.

Minds On!

Have you ever watched the clouds float across the sky? Can you predict the weather from your observations? What type of cloud are you observing on a foggy morning? What weather will this type of cloud bring?●

TRY THIS

Activity!

Cloud Watching

Can you predict what tomorrow's weather will be by observing clouds?

What You Need
cotton balls, construction paper, glue, *Activity Log* page 14

From a window in your classroom, observe the clouds you can see. Use the cotton balls to make a model of the clouds you observe. Predict what you think tomorrow's weather will be based on the clouds you observe. Be sure to add these observations to your *Activity Log.* Check your prediction the next day.

Focus
on
Environment

Rain Shadow

Water is necessary for plants and animals to live and grow. Some areas of the world have lots of water. Other areas have little water because they get little rain. Some areas that are separated from an ocean by high mountains get little rainfall.

> The air that moves over the mountain has little moisture left.

> The water vapor in this air condenses and clouds form.

> Rain or snow falls on the side of the mountain facing the ocean.

> Moist air moving onto the land rises up the sides of the mountains. As it moves upward, it cools.

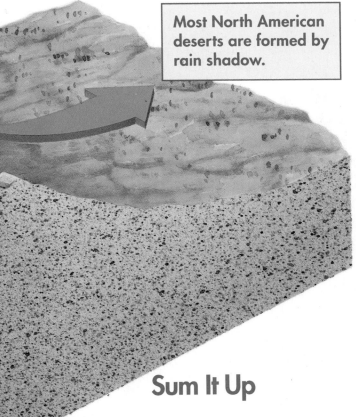

The land on the side of the mountain away from the ocean gets little rain. This area is called a **rain shadow,** a type of desert.

Most North American deserts are formed by rain shadow.

Making Deserts Green?

A **desert** is an area of land that receives less than 25 centimeters (about 10 inches) of rainfall per year. Very few plants grow in deserts because of the lack of water. In some places people have made desert areas green. They do this by bringing water to these areas. Watering this land by artificial methods is called **irrigation** (ir´ i gā´ shən). About 220 million **hectares** (about 550 million acres) of land are being irrigated around the world. In some countries more water is used for irrigation than for any other purpose.

Sum It Up

Understanding the water cycle will help you understand weather and how it changes. The water cycle is one of the cycles that are found in the different systems that form weather. For example, most storms are the result of the way that wind systems and water systems work together. Violent storms such as hurricanes bring both strong winds and heavy rains.

Critical Thinking

1. Why does fog often form early in the morning?

2. Why is your breath visible in cold weather?

3. On a hot day, someone sees you fanning yourself with a paper fan. This person says, "You're only making yourself hotter." How do you respond?

Why Does the Weather Change?

Whether the weather be fine
Or whether the weather be not
Whether the weather be cold
Or whether the weather be hot,
We'll weather the weather
Whatever the weather,
Whether we like it or not.

Changing weather in Loudoun County, Virginia, United States

Scientists who study the weather and prepare weather reports are called **meteorologists** (mē´ tē ə rol´ ə jists). One condition meteorologists use to help them forecast weather is air pressure. In the following activity, you will have a chance to make and use an instrument meteorologists use.

Activity!

Getting in Front of Weather Changes

In this activity you will make a weather instrument called a barometer and use it to observe changes in air pressure for four days. Using the barometer will help you predict the weather.

What You Need

Activity Log pages 15-16

safety goggles

1 lb. coffee can

index card

rubber band

marker

balloon

tape

drinking straw

scissors

thermometer

What To Do

1 Cut the balloon just above the point where the neck ends. Stretch the balloon tightly over the open top of the can. Hold the balloon in place with a rubber band. *Safety Tip:* Wear safety goggles when using a rubber band.

2 Lay the drinking straw on the balloon so that about one-third of the straw sticks out beyond the edge of the can. Attach the straw to the balloon with a strip of transparent tape.

See the *Safety Tip* in step 1.

3 Hold the index card lengthwise and write HIGHER at the top of the card and LOWER at the bottom of the card. Now fold the card lengthwise about 1 cm. Put a piece of masking tape on the fold and tape it just behind the part of the straw that is hanging over the edge of the can. At the end of the straw, mark the index card with a heavy black line and write DAY 1 next to the line.

4 Set up the thermometer near the barometer.

5 At the same time each day, mark the position of the straw on the card with a heavy black line and write DAY 2, DAY 3, DAY 4 so that you can see if the straw went up or down. Each day, record whether the pressure is rising or falling. Record the air temperature, sky color, clouds, and wind speed. Compare your observations with a newspaper or television weather report.

What Happened?

1. What happened to make your barometer record a high pressure on the card?

2. What type of weather did you see on days with high air pressure? What type of weather did you see on days with low air pressure?

3. Based on your observations in this activity, predict what weather conditions will be like on the fifth day.

What Now?

1. How accurate were your weather predictions?

2. What connection did you notice between air pressure and temperature?

3. What type of reading would you expect from your barometer if warm air were to move into your area?

EXPLORE

49

Air Masses and Fronts

Your barometer showed you changes in air pressure. When the air pressure fell, your barometer read lower. High air pressure made your barometer read higher.

Weather (weth´ ər) is the condition of the atmosphere at a particular time and place. When weather forecasters predict weather, they track the movement of air masses. An **air mass** is a large body of air with nearly the same temperature and moisture throughout. Air masses may form over either water or land. They take on the properties of the surfaces they form over.

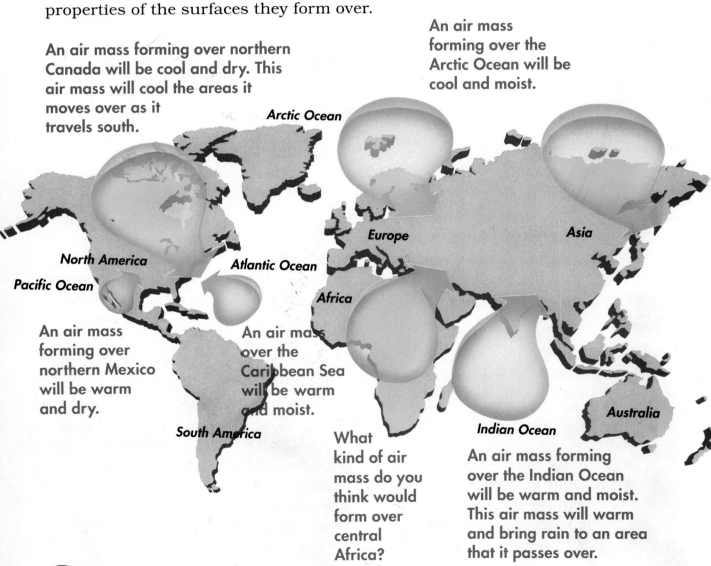

An air mass forming over northern Canada will be cool and dry. This air mass will cool the areas it moves over as it travels south.

An air mass forming over the Arctic Ocean will be cool and moist.

Arctic Ocean

Europe

Asia

North America

Atlantic Ocean

Africa

Pacific Ocean

An air mass forming over northern Mexico will be warm and dry.

An air mass over the Caribbean Sea will be warm and moist.

South America

What kind of air mass do you think would form over central Africa?

Indian Ocean

Australia

An air mass forming over the Indian Ocean will be warm and moist. This air mass will warm and bring rain to an area that it passes over.

Air masses move as the wind blows. When they move, they bump into or push against other air masses. Air masses usually do not mix because of differences in air pressure and temperature. The place where two different air masses meet is called a **front**. Most of our storms form along fronts.

A cold air mass moves through warm air.

A **cold front** often produces fast-rising air and strong winds. The dense cold mass slides under the less dense warm mass. This front may produce thunderstorms.

A warm air mass moves in an area of cool air.

Cirrus clouds may tell you a **warm front** is coming. In a warm front warm air rises up and over the denser cold air.

TRY THIS

Activity!

Move Aside, Here I Come!

You are going to see how a front forms by using cold water and hot water.

What You Need
clear plastic shoe box, heavy piece of cardboard, red food coloring, blue food coloring, 16-oz. jar of very hot water, 16-oz. jar of very cold water, *Activity Log* page 17

Cut a heavy piece of cardboard so that it is exactly as wide as the shoe box. Place the cardboard across the middle of the shoe box vertically so that it divides the shoe box in half. It must fit very snugly. Ask your partner to hold the cardboard firmly in place. Put 5 drops of red food coloring in the jar of hot water that you have. Put 5 drops of blue food coloring in the jar of cold water. Swirl the jars to mix the food coloring with the water. *Safety Tip:* Pour the red water into one side of the box with care. Pour the blue water into the other side of the box. Have your partner quickly pull the cardboard straight up and out of the shoe box. What happened? Record your observations.

Thunderstorms

Minds On! Think about the last rainstorm in your area. Was the rain light and steady or heavy with strong winds, thunder, and lightning?

Rainstorms or snowstorms can happen when two air masses meet along a front. When the warm, humid air along a front is pushed up suddenly, a thunderstorm may develop.

As the warm air rises, it cools, and the water vapor condenses and forms a dark **thundercloud**. As more air is pushed up along the front, the cloud grows taller, forming a **thunderhead**.

Thunderheads can produce strong lightning, thunder, and heavy rains. Sometimes the water droplets fall to Earth as hail. Hail forms when water droplets in the thunderhead are moved quickly up and down through layers of cold air. The drops freeze into ice crystals and grow large enough to fall to the ground as lumps of ice.

Most thunderstorms in the United States occur from May through September. Thunderstorms can be very dangerous because the lightning that is produced from these storms can cause injury and sometimes death. Follow these safety tips if you know a thunderstorm is coming.

Weather   Literature Link

Read about severe weather storms in *Weather* by Howard E. Smith. As you read, make a list of the types of severe storms that occur in the world in your ***Activity Log*** on page 18. When you have finished reading, number the list of storms from most severe to least severe. Discuss the reasons for your choices with your classmates.

Never stand under a lone tree in an open field because lightning strikes the highest point around.

Don't stay outside during a storm. Go inside a large building or car to protect yourself from lightning.

Don't take a bath or shower. Stay away from water taps and sinks. Minerals in water conduct electricity from lightning, which could shock you.

Don't talk on the telephone unless it's an emergency. Telephone wires conduct electricity, and you could get a shock.

Tornadoes

The wind and lightning in thunderstorms can be very dangerous, but other storms can be even more violent. The **tornado** (tôr nā´ dō) is a rapidly circling column of air that moves in a narrow path over land. A tornado that is still in the air is called a funnel cloud.

A tornado can reach wind speeds of up to 418 kilometers (about 260 miles) per hour. It can pull up trees and tear apart buildings. Cars and trees have been lifted and carried through the air for hundreds of meters. Tornadoes kill many people because they appear so quickly and with less warning than other kinds of storms. A tornado is dangerous because it moves in an unpredictable path.

Tornadoes form in severe thunderstorms that contain rising warm air.

When the warm air rises in the back of the storm, it draws cool air from the bottom of the storm and forms funnel clouds.

Funnel clouds that touch the ground are called tornadoes.

More tornadoes occur in the United States than in any other country, especially in the area of the United States called Tornado Alley.

Tornadoes form when air masses of different temperatures collide. Most tornadoes occur from April through July. In the summer, in the states along Tornado Alley, hot land areas may warm up air masses throughout the day. In the late afternoon, as the temperature cools, cooler air masses may move in. Steep thunderheads will form along the cold front. Some thunderheads may extend upward to 1,825 meters (about 5,986 feet). In a thunderstorm system of this size, tornadoes may occur.

Hurricanes

If you live in a coastal area, you may have to prepare for hurricanes. A **hurricane** (hûr´ i kān´) is a violent storm that forms over a warm ocean. The official hurricane season in the United States is June 1 through November 30.

Winds swirl around the *eye*, or center, of the hurricane. The eye is actually a calm area with few clouds in which the sun may be shining. The eye measures about 32 kilometers (about 20 miles) in diameter.

Winds near the center of a hurricane range in speed from 119 to 322 kilometers (about 74 to 200 miles) per hour.

Hurricanes form in areas of low pressure over warm water. Although they develop and pick up speed over water, hurricanes often move inland, away from the water.

A hurricane usually measures from 322 to 805 kilometers (about 200 to 500 miles) in diameter.

When hurricanes move over coastal areas, the waves, tides, winds, and rain can cause enormous damage. The damage from a hurricane can extend over an area hundreds of kilometers from its center.

Wall clouds surround the eye of the hurricane. These clouds have the strongest winds and heaviest rain of the hurricane.

Hurricane!

Literature Link

Read Faith McNulty's book *Hurricane!* In your **Activity Log** on page 19, make a list of all the things John, his family, and the community do to prepare for the hurricane. Think about the kinds of buildings described in the book and what happens to them. What types of buildings can withstand hurricanes? What kinds of structures exist where you live? Add anything else you think you would need to do to prepare your home for a hurricane.

All in a Day's Work

Meteorologists around the world work together to share weather information gathered from satellites, weather balloons, radar, weather stations, aircraft, and computers.

Airline pilots radio air traffic control centers with the weather conditions of the air they are flying through.

Meteorologists use computers to gather weather data and make five-day forecasts.

All around the world, gas-filled weather balloons are launched at midnight and midday to take measurements of air pressure, temperature, humidity, and wind speed at different levels of Earth's atmosphere.

Weather stations are used around the world to collect weather information every hour. Meteorologists use the data on wind speed and direction, air pressure, temperature, humidity, and precipitation to prepare forecasts.

There are two kinds of weather satellites that monitor cloud formations around the world. Meteorologists can predict what kind of weather is coming from the pictures sent back to Earth.

TRY THIS Activity! *Forecasting the Weather*

What You Need
4 days of newspaper weather maps, *Activity Log* page 20

A study of weather maps shows that weather fronts in the United States usually move from west to east. Use the newspaper weather maps to track an air mass in the United States for three days. In your **Activity Log,** record which states the air mass covered on each day. Write down if it is a warm or a cold air mass. Note any changes in size.

Predict where the air mass will move on the fourth day by drawing a map of the area it will cover. Prepare a weather forecast for that area. Compare your drawing with the newspaper map. How good was your weather forecasting?

Stormy Weather Worldwide

People around the world use many different words for the same weather conditions, especially for violent storms and winds.

Cyclone (sī´ klōn) comes from the Greek word *kykloein* (kü´ klō ān´), meaning "moving in a circle" or "whirling." In a cyclone, winds rotate around a moving center of low air pressure. Because of Earth's rotation, cyclones spin clockwise in the Southern Hemisphere and counterclockwise in the Northern Hemisphere. Hurricanes that form in the Indian Ocean are called cyclones.

Typhoon (tī fün´) takes us to the other side of the globe. It is from a Chinese word meaning "great wind." Hurricanes that form in the Pacific Ocean are called typhoons.

Monsoon (mon sün´) comes originally from an Arabic word meaning "season." Monsoons are the winds in the Indian Ocean that change direction with the season. They are very powerful, bring rain, and determine the time when the people can plant crops.

Santa Ana (san´ tə an´ ə) winds are named for the community of Santa Ana, California. They occur during the winter. They blow across the mountains from the deserts and plateaus of lower east California, carrying dust particles. They are hot and dry, and because they are so strong, they often make forest fires difficult to stop.

Sum It Up

The weather is always changing. Air masses and fronts move across Earth to cause all types of weather. The patterns of weather that forecasters track, plus weather instruments like barometers that forecasters use, work together to help people prepare for life-threatening storms as well as everyday weather.

Critical Thinking

1. What happens when two air masses meet?

2. How does a thunderhead develop?

3. How are tornadoes and hurricanes alike? How are they different?

Weather, Climate, and You

Do you have a different set of clothes for each season? Or can you wear the same type of clothing year-round? The weather and climate where you live affect what you do and what you wear all year long.

In some areas you can play on a beach in the winter.

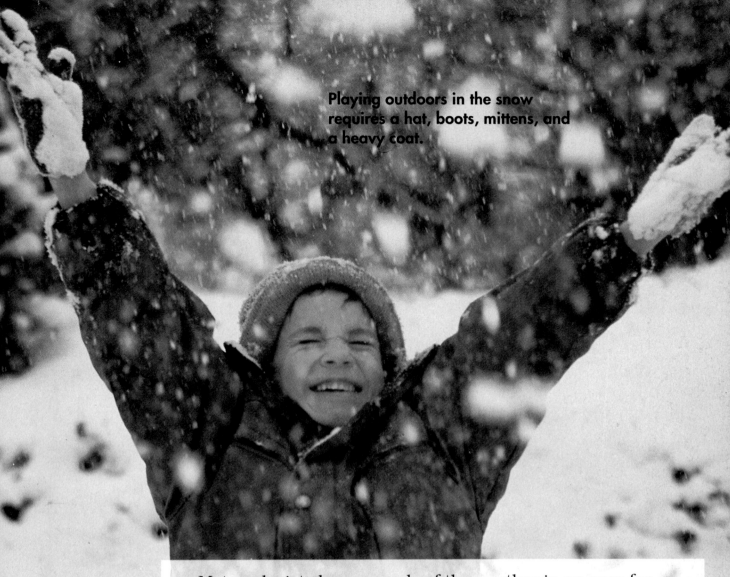

Playing outdoors in the snow requires a hat, boots, mittens, and a heavy coat.

Meteorologists keep records of the weather in an area for about 30 years. They watch to see what kinds of weather occur over and over again. We call the pattern of weather in an area year after year the **climate** (klīˊ mit). Climate affects your life in many ways. One of those ways is the clothing you wear. For example, if you live in Maine, you will need a heavy coat, mittens, boots, and a hat if you plan to play outdoors in the winter. If you live in Southern California, you might wear a light shirt and shorts in February!

You have been learning about weather conditions that happen day by day. Now you will study weather that happens over a longer period of time.

Activity!

Discovering Climate in North America

Many different climates exist in North America. You are going to investigate one area in North America and identify the type of climate in that area.

What You Need

Activity Log pages 21-22

travel brochures from U.S., Canada, and Mexico

worksheet

encyclopedia

almanac

glue

crayons

scissors

What To Do

1 Look at the map of North America.

2 Color the zone marked *number 1*, blue. Color the zone marked *number 2*, green. Color the zone marked *number 3*, red.

3 Choose one of the areas that you just colored. Use the encyclopedia or travel brochures to find the average summer temperature and the average winter temperature in your zone of climate.

4 Use the encyclopedia or almanac to find the average yearly rainfall for your area.

5 Use the encyclopedia or travel brochures to find out what kinds of plants grow in your climate. Draw three kinds in your *Activity Log.*

6 Use the encyclopedia or travel brochures to find out what kinds of animals live in your climate zone. Draw one animal in your *Activity Log* or cut out a picture of one from a travel brochure.

What Happened?

1. What zone of climate would be the best for people who like winter sports?

2. Which zone of climate would be the best for farming?

3. How does the weather affect the way people live and work in the zone of climate you chose?

What Now?

1. What would happen to your area if the average yearly temperature increased?

2. What would happen to your area if the average yearly temperature decreased?

3. Does being close to or far away from the equator make a difference in the type of climate that an area has? Explain why you think so.

EXPLORE

World Climates

In the Explore Activity, you discovered that climate has an effect on plants, animals, and people. It makes a difference in the types of houses that people live in, the clothing they wear, the type of food they grow, and the jobs they do.

Laplanders live in a type of climate with long, bitterly cold winters and short, cool summers. Reindeer are raised for food and transportation.

Bedouins live in the deserts of the Middle East. They may live in tents and travel frequently to find water and grass for their camels, sheep, and goats.

People who live by the Mediterranean Sea usually have mild, rainy winters and hot summers. Anchovies, sardines, shrimp, and tuna are caught in the waters of the Mediterranean.

The Senegalese live on the tropical coast of Africa. The weather is usually warm and moist year-round.

Minds On! Waynesburg, Pennsylvania, celebrates an interesting festival each July 29 called "Rain Day." Why is it always on July 29? No one knows why, but it has rained 95 out of the last 115 years on July 29. Sometimes it is just a sprinkle or two. Sometimes a downpour can rain the festival out! If you were going to celebrate a festival that was all about climate, what would it be? ●

Social Studies Link

Let Us Plant Lettuce!

Have you ever helped someone plant seeds in a garden or a window box? What do you remember about the back of the seed package? Those multicolored maps are actually climate maps. The bands of color on the maps show the best time to plant the seeds in the packet for every area of the United States. The colors also show the last likely date for **frost** in an area. Farmers and gardeners need to know the frost date because frost will kill many vegetable and flower plants. What are the frost dates for your area? Can you grow vegetables year-round?

Seasons and Climates

You have learned that average temperature is related to geographic location. The way that Earth orbits around the sun should make this more clear for you.

Earth's axis is an imaginary line that runs through its center. The axis is always tilted in the same direction in space.

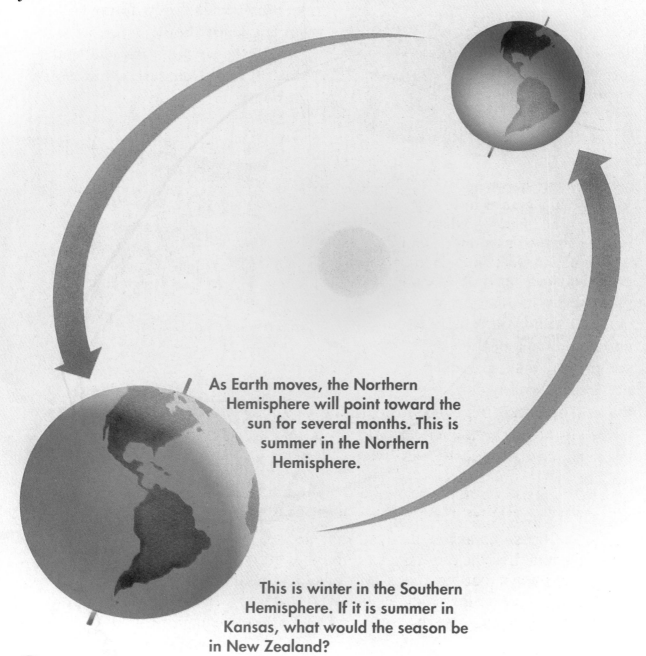

As Earth moves, the Northern Hemisphere will point toward the sun for several months. This is summer in the Northern Hemisphere.

This is winter in the Southern Hemisphere. If it is summer in Kansas, what would the season be in New Zealand?

Illustration not drawn to scale.

Climate Zones

Earth has three basic climate zones—polar, tropical, and temperate. What climate zone do you live in?

Places closest to the equator have **tropical** climates. They are warm or hot year-round because they receive intense energy from the sun every day.

Places that are between the equator and the poles have **temperate** climates, which means that the weather is warmer than in the polar zone but cooler than in the tropical zone of climate.

Polar climates are cold and occur in regions that don't receive sunlight as directly as the tropical zone does.

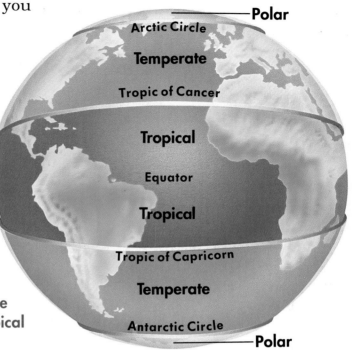

Polar

Arctic Circle

Temperate

Tropic of Cancer

Tropical

Equator

Tropical

Tropic of Capricorn

Temperate

Antarctic Circle

Polar

TRY THIS Activity! *Polar Zebra*

You have probably seen pictures of animals that live in a tropical climate. What would happen if a zebra or an elephant went to the North Pole to live?

What You Need
crayons, magazines or books with animal pictures, *Activity Log* page 23

Choose an animal that you know lives in a warm, tropical climate. Use the magazines or books to see where it lives. Think of three ways that the animal will have to adapt to a new, polar climate. Write the changes in your *Activity Log.* Draw a picture of the animal you have chosen in its new environment.

Repairing the Ozone

One place where scientists have carefully studied the atmosphere is over Antarctica. Some scientists are concerned about the holes that are growing in the ozone layer. **Ozone** (ō´ zōn) is a form of oxygen that can be found in the stratosphere. The ozone layer keeps out most of the sun's harmful **ultraviolet** (ul´ trə vī´ ə lit) rays, which can cause skin cancer. Scientists are also studying the effect of the holes on Earth's climate.

Antarctica

Scientists have found that the holes are caused by chemical compounds called **chlorofluorocarbons** (klôr´ ə flôr´ ə kär´ bənz) or CFCs. CFCs are used in refrigerators and in air conditioners for homes and cars. The United States and many other countries want CFCs to be eliminated in all products by the year 2000.

Aerosol cans, like the one shown here, contain CFCs, which harm the atmosphere. Most products now use air pump sprays.

Blocking Out the Sun

When you go outside to play on a sunny day, do you put sunblock on your face? Do you wear a hat? Do you rest in the shade or under an umbrella? Scientists are concerned about the amount of ultraviolet rays that come through the holes in the ozone layer because these rays can cause sunburn and dangerous skin cancers. Sunscreen products that say 15 or 40 on the front will give you 15 or 40 times more protection from the sun than not using any protection at all. However, recent studies have shown that sunscreens can prevent sunburn but may not be able to prevent skin cancer. So be smart and don't overdo your time in the sun.

Always wear a sunscreen outdoors.

Sum It Up

Earth's climates are the result of many factors that work together. The climate where you live is a result of the weather that has happened for a long time, the distance you are from the equator, Earth's tilt, and whether you live near a large body of water or near mountains or hills. Where you live affects the way you live. How does climate affect your life?

Critical Thinking

1. Geographical location is important to the climate of an area. Think of some landforms that influence your climate.

2. How do air temperature and ground surface work together to cause climate?

3. Draw three ways that people can affect the climate around them. Make your drawings colorful and eye-catching.

Understanding Air, Weather, and Climate

You know that weather and climate are both caused by the interaction between the sun and Earth. The daily changes that take place in the troposphere are called weather. Climate is the average weather of an area measured over a longer period of time. What do weather and climate have in common? Wind, temperature, and water are three important conditions for weather and climate.

Worldwide Weather Disasters

Social Studies Link

You have seen that weather can be unpredictable even though meteorologists have the most modern scientific equipment to track storms around the world. Here are some weather disasters that happened from 1737 to the present day. After you have read the time line, decide if you think any of these events could have been prevented. Choose one of the events on the time line and find out more about the disaster. What makes one disaster worse than another?

1737 India

A giant storm surge caused by a tropical cyclone swept away everything in its path on the Hooghly (hū´ lē) River.

1876–1879 China

Crop failure caused by lack of rain resulted in the Great Famine.

1899 United States

A dam at the head of the South Fork Reservoir, in a valley of the Allegheny Mountains, burst after a long period of rain and flooded Johnstown, Pennsylvania.

1954 Austria

An avalanche traveling at a speed of more than 320 kilometers (about 200 miles) per hour roared down Mt. Montcalv (män käl´) and buried the town of Blons (blônz).

1954 Haiti

Hurricane Hazel blew winds of over 192 kilometers (about 119 miles) per hour over Haiti's southern coast.

1962 Peru

Unusually warm temperatures melted a glacier on top of Nevado Huascaran (nā vä´ do hwa skä rän´). A wall of ice and snow crashed down on the town of Ranrahirca (rän rä´ hîr kä) at more than 161 kilometers (about 100 miles) per hour.

1991 Bangladesh (bang glə desh´)

Islands were covered by a 6-meter (about 20 feet) tidal wave.

Activity!

As the World Turns

Climate is different all around the world. What makes it that way? Read these interesting facts about climate. Write your answers to the following questions in your **Activity Log.**

What You Need

meter tape, atlas, globe,
Activity Log page 24

Greatest number of thunderstorm days: Kampala, Uganda 242 thunderstorm days per year

What do you think the climate is like in Kampala?

Greatest rainfall in one year: 2,602 centimeters Assam, India August 1860 to August 1861

With the meter tape, measure out 2,602 centimeters. Where do you think all the water would go?

World's worst tornado: Tri-State Tornado
Missouri, Illinois, Indiana, United States
March 18, 1925

Name three modern ways to predict tornadoes that would have prevented so many people from being killed in this tornado in 1925.

Greatest snowfall in 24 hours: 189.5 centimeters
Silver Lake, Colorado
April 14–15, 1921

Look out your classroom window and describe what would be buried under 189.5 centimeters of snow!

Longest period without rain: 400 years
The desert of Atacama, Chile

Notice the land features of Chile. Explain why Atacama has not had rain in over 400 years. What kind of life do you think exists in the desert?

Longest hot spell: 38°C for 162 consecutive days
Marble Bar, Western Australia
October 31, 1923, to April 7, 1924

What kinds of activities could you do if there were no air conditioning or public pools to keep you cool during a heat wave?

Minds On! Imagine you could choose to live in any area on Earth. Where do you think is the perfect place? List three reasons for choosing this area. Describe the climate of your new home in a picture.●

GLOSSARY

Use the pronunciation key below to help you decode, or read, the pronunciations.

Pronunciation Key

a	at, bad	d	dear, soda, bad
ā	ape, pain, day, break	f	five, defend, leaf, off, cough, elephant
ä	father, car, heart	g	game, ago, fog, egg
âr	care, pair, bear, their, where	h	hat, ahead
e	end, pet, said, heaven, friend	hw	white, whether, which
ē	equal, me, feet, team, piece, key	j	joke, enjoy, gem, page, edge
i	it, big, English, hymn	k	kite, bakery, seek, tack, cat
ī	ice, fine, lie, my	l	lid, sailor, feel, ball, allow
îr	ear, deer, here, pierce	m	man, family, dream
o	odd, hot, watch	n	not, final, pan, knife
ō	old, oat, toe, low	ng	long, singer, pink
ô	coffee, all, taught, law, fought	p	pail, repair, soap, happy
ôr	order, fork, horse, story, pour	r	ride, parent, wear, more, marry
oi	oil, toy	s	sit, aside, pets, cent, pass
ou	out, now	sh	shoe, washer, fish mission, nation
u	up, mud, love, double	t	tag, pretend, fat, button, dressed
ū	use, mule, cue, feud, few	th	thin, panther, both
ü	rule, true, food	<u>th</u>	this, mother, smooth
ů	put, wood, should	v	very, favor, wave
ûr	burn, hurry, term, bird, word, courage	w	wet, weather, reward
ə	about, taken, pencil, lemon, circus	y	yes, onion
b	bat, above, job	z	zoo, lazy, jazz, rose, dogs, houses
ch	chin, such, match	zh	vision, treasure, seizure

air mass (âr mas) a body of air with about the same temperature, humidity, and pressure

air pressure (âr presh´ər) the pressure exerted in all directions by air pressing on an object

anemometer (an´ə mom´i tər) weather instrument that measures wind speed

atmosphere (at´məs fîr´) gases surrounding Earth

barometer (bə rom´i tər) instrument for measuring air pressure

blimp (blimp) airship with no rigid framework

chlorofluorocarbon (klôr´ə flür ə kär´bən) any of various compounds made of carbon, chlorine, fluorine, and sometimes hydrogen

cirrus (sir´əs) white, wispy, high-level cloud made up of ice crystals

climate (klī´mit) the typical weather conditions of a particular place over a long period of time

cloud (kloud) a mass of water droplets and/or ice particles floating in the air

cold front (kōld frunt) the forward edge of a mass of cold air moving into an area of warmer air

condensation (kon´den sā´shən) the change of a gas into a liquid or solid

cumulus (kū´myə ləs) a dense cloud made up of billowing mounds

cyclone (sī´klōn) a disturbance in the atmosphere in which winds rotate around a low air pressure center

dense (dens) having parts closely packed together

desert (dez´ərt) region with less than 25 centimeters (about 10 inches) of rainfall annually

evaporation (i vap´ə rā´shən) the change of a liquid into a gas

front (frunt) the boundary between two air masses of different temperature

frost (frôst) tiny ice crystals that form when water vapor changes directly to ice on the surface of exposed objects

global warming (glō´bəl wôrm´ing) a rise in Earth's average temperatures

greenhouse effect (grēn´hous´ i fekt´) a warming process in which the sun's heat is temporarily trapped in the atmosphere by certain atmospheric gases such as water vapor, carbon dioxide, and methane

hectare (hek´târ) a unit of area in the metric system, equal to 10,000 square meters or about 2½ acres

hurricane (hûr´i kān´) a storm of tropical origin with winds of about 121 kilometers (about 75 miles) per hour or more in the Atlantic and Caribbean regions

ionosphere (ī on´ə sfir´) an area of ionized gases high in Earth's atmosphere

irrigation (ir´i gā´shən) bringing water to crops by artificial means

mass (mas) the amount of matter in an object

mesosphere (mez´ə sfir´) the layer of Earth's atmosphere above the stratosphere

meteorologist (mē´tē ə rol´ə jist) a scientist who studies the weather

monsoon (mon sün) a seasonally varying wind of the Indian Ocean and southern Asia.

ozone (ō´zōn) a form of oxygen that is a pale blue gas with a distinctive odor

ozone layer (ō´zōn lā´ər) a layer of ozone in the stratosphere which absorbs ultraviolet rays, preventing them from reaching Earth

precipitation (pri sip´i tā´shən) any form of water that falls to Earth

rain shadow (rān shad´ō) a dry area on the downward side of a mountain

Santa Ana (San´tə an´ə) seasonal winds that blow in California

stratosphere (strat´ə sfir´) the layer of the atmosphere above the troposphere, where a major ozone layer occurs

stratus (stra´təs) a low-level gray cloud that has a flat, layered form

thundercloud (thun´dər kloud) a large, dark cloud charged with electricity and producing thunder and lightning

thunderhead (thun´dər hed) upper portion of a thundercloud

tornado (tôr nā´dō) severe funnel shaped storm in which winds blow very rapidly around an area of very low pressure

transpiration (tran´spə rā´shən) the process by which plants transfer water vapor to the atmosphere

troposphere (trop´ə sfir´) the layer of the atmosphere closest to Earth

warm front (wôrm frunt) the forward edge of a mass of warm air that is rising over a mass of cold air

water cycle (wô´tər sī´kəl) the continuous movement of water in the environment through evaporation, condensation, and precipitation

weather (weth´ər) the day to day conditions in the atmosphere, such as temperature, wind speed and direction, air pressure, humidity, and precipitation

wind (wind) air moving through the atmosphere

INDEX

CREDITS